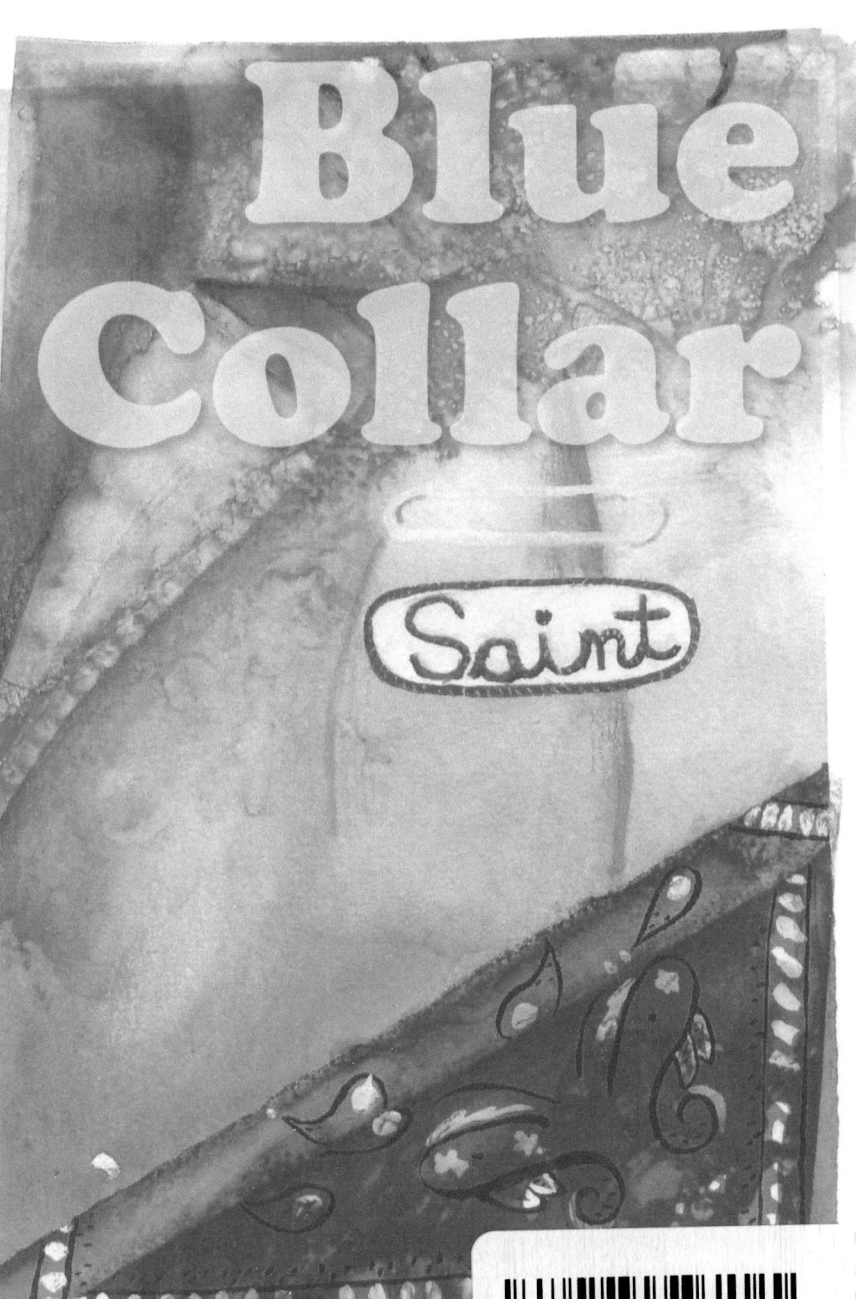

Blue Collar Saint

Poems by

Brenda Leigh White

Meadowlark Press
Emporia, Kansas, USA

Meadowlark Press, LLC
Meadowlark Poetry Press
meadowlark-books.com
P.O. Box 333, Emporia, KS 66801

Blue Collar Saint
Copyright © Brenda Leigh White, 2021

Cover image by Lacy Auchard.

All rights reserved. This book or any portion thereof
may not be reproduced or used in any manner whatsoever
without the express written permission of the author
except for the use of brief quotations in a book review.

ISBN: 978-1-7362232-8-4

Library of Congress Control Number: 2021948067

*For Curtis Becker who saved my life,
and for my family who put up with
my poetic sensibilities*

Contents

I. The White White House

The White White House /3
July 4, 2019 /6
My Vietnam Experience /7
February 13, 2017 /8
Half Baked /9
Beauty Queen Never /11
9/11 /12
Hymn for Gen X and Millennials /13
In the Town of Knife /14
Blue Collar Saint /15
Flight or Fight /17
Covid-19 2020 /18
Changelings /19
To Kate Spade /20

II. Praise the Lord and Pass the Medication

Amitriptyline /23
Abilify /24
Wellbutrin /25
Cymbalta /26
Reckless Driving /27
I Was Here /28
Escape Artist /29
Solar-Powered /30
Catnapping /31
My Favorite Pair of Shoes /32
Mended /33

God Makes Mistakes   /34
Gay   /35
Leznupar   /36
Bound for Extinction   /37
Note Left on the Kitchen Table for My Family   /38

III. Marked on God's Atomic Map

Turkeys Traverse Timber   /41
Controlled Burn   /42
After the Service   /43
Family Photo   /45
Hackberry Emperors   /46
My Toad   /47
Hearts Are the Most Useless Things   /48
Going Home   /49
Recalling Grandma in the West Timber   /50
September   /51
Seagulls in Kansas   /52
Fall Memory   /53
Unintended   /54
Tiny Miracles   /55
Oriole   /57

IV. Thirty Day Chip

Far Side Love at World's End   /61
To the Moon   /62
Spaghetti Supper Tango   /63
Blank When it Comes to Verse   /65
To the People Who Lost One Shoe   /66
Haiku   /68
February 2, 2020   /69
Mardi Gras 2020   /70
Memorial Day 2019   /71

Monday Evening at Writers' Group   /72
Breaking Writer's Block   /75
Dear Autocorrect   /76
Tuffy on Sunday Morning   /77
Tempests and Teacups   /78
Fools and Money   /79
Tenacity   /80

V. Stardust

Palmystery   /83
Prayer to My Angels   /85
If You Believe in ME—Let Go   /86
Indifference   /87
Afternoon Visit   /88
Lost in Translation   /89
Doll Dreams and Handmade Wishes   /91
Fallen   /92
Fire Sign (Leo Super Moon)   /93
Full Pink Moon   /94
Stardust   /95
Damned   /96
Psychic Lace   /98
Heartbreak in Heaven   /99
Bread of Life   /100

About the Author   /103
About the Cover Artist   /103
Acknowledgments   /105

I.
The White White House

The White White House

My father, the retired machinist, has decided to run for President.
If elected, he won't wear neck ties and will leave his shirt
unbuttoned at the collar.

He plans to keep Sarah Huckabee Sanders as his Press Secretary.
She will explain the President does not intend to choke,
and as for his lack of ties, he wants all
males in his presence to suffer no feelings of
inadequacy when they discover in which
direction neck ties point.

There will be a flat tax for everyone,
no deductions, and all individuals,
including corporations, will pay their full amount—
cash, no I.O.U.s, handshakes, or payment plans.

State dinners will consist of large steaks, rare,
baked potatoes, asparagus, and broccoli.
Perhaps the occasional pork roast.
Dessert will be Oreos and milk or Diet Coke.

Ms. Sanders says the President fully supports
cattlemen, meat packing plants, and Idaho.

Should Vladmir Putin declare war on the U.S.,
the President will say, "I hope you brought your lunch."
Ms. Sanders doesn't bat an eye, blink, or cough.
"Our President remains firm with enemies of the State.
His policy is always transparency."

There will be a resumption of public floggings for politicians who lie,
provided their actions have severely vexed the Commander in Chief.
He will spank them, televised live, with his own belt
as he tells them, "It hurts me more than you."

Unfortunately, flatulence may be prevalent during Presidential
    addresses.
Ms. Sanders will respond that the President has
bad gut feelings about most issues, and
cushioned mats will be provided for press members close to the
    podium.
All other journalists will be blamed for further
excessive intestinal emissions and
advised by Ms. Sanders to use Beano.

"Clearly the Press remains a danger to the Public
and an enemy to common decency,"
to which the President will reply,

"Pull my finger."

Asked about his Platform, my father of our country will say,
"I want it made of wood."
I will advise him, as First Daughter,
that he must rescind the tariffs of his predecessor.
His girth will require steel for total support.
"All terrorists must die!" the President avers.
"That's tariffs, dad," I correct.

Ms. Sanders will announce in her next release
"The President does have some hearing challenges.
Please, everyone, look him in the face and annunciate.
We appreciate your cooperation."

As tools have been known to fly in the machine shop,
my father's incumbency may include occasional projectiles:
ink pens, wadded up accords, podiums, perhaps congresspersons.
Should anything be broken during these exertions,
he will turn to my mother and Ms. Sanders,
warning through gritted teeth,
"Don't say a word, not one word."

Despite his few foibles, as leader of our nation
my father will enhance White House security
in the personage of the First Lady.
They will be late to every Presidential engagement
as my mother will insist on double and
triple checks that ensure
the windows and doors are locked,
the stove burners are all off,
the toaster is unplugged,

and the cat is not locked in a bathroom.

As for myself, I intend to spend the totality of my father's term
in the White House broom closet.
Equipped with a hot tub and large screen television,
I will remain with my dog and several cats,
drinking margaritas and eating chocolate
until it is safe to return to the
remnants of our former lives.

July 4, 2019

My dog and I huddle in the living room
while neighbors assault the atmosphere.
Their banshee fountains wail and whistle.
The hollow plonft of their Roman candles
arc orbs of red, green, blue,
then fade and float to earth.
Rib-vibrating cannons blast
microstars to Heaven
that pop or shrill, or buzz like swirling bees,
dissipate in puffs of colored smoke,
all to celebrate a middle finger
extended to a king.

The noise goes on and on
and each explosion chings
a cash register button
in my mind.
How much money did
they give to China to
celebrate being free?

Rebels without a clue.
Rent and utilities will yet be due.

In the morning
when the smoke clears
over ramparts and rooftops
and the bills are paid,
I hope we all still have our
freedom.

Brenda Leigh White

My Vietnam Experience

Vietnam was black and white
and 26 inches at news time.

Reporters embedded in fighting, in foliage,
shouted body counts above machine gun fire,
helicopter rotors, random grenades.

Cameras panned bodies with slanted eyes
tossed amid the grey leaves and vines.

I was too young to fathom flies or
understand the stench of rotting flesh,
to comprehend pointlessness and
price of Police Actions,
to picture any of it in color.

Instead, I believed a Green Beret's
wish for silver wings pinned on his son's chest.
I even sang along.

On the radio, Glenn Campbell
longed for a beautiful girl on a sun-drenched beach,
aimed his gun, and dreamed of
Galveston.

February 13, 2017

In Delphi, Indiana, they need an oracle
or a miracle to find a monster
meandering their woods,
that fiend in human disguise who
mumbles, ". . . down the hill . . ."
to little girls he rapes and mutilates.

I would volunteer to isolate,
stand over a crevice and
breathe in rotting stench,
scry a bowl of spring water,
render a name or visage,
his lair.

Leave it to the Lord, some say,
His judgment is best,
but I am tired of waiting on Him,
His days so long compared to mine.

They need a handmaiden of justice
not afraid to perceive evil through
mist and smoke,
someone to remind us with her ravings
two souls deserve accountability,
that monsters having tasted flesh
need slain before preying again.

Half Baked

Are we done yet, Sylvia?
A timer bzzzz
and no one to turn it off.

Too bad my stove is electric,
hot air without fumes
save fried hair
and my smile melting
at 400 degrees.

I could write, "I was here,"
in blots of fruit pies past.

We both know life is
not a gas,
but sometimes a place to rest
one's head is easy as
opening an oven door.

My old bean is heavy as
pot roast.

Given time, could we rise
like bread dough
or cinnamon rolls?

I'm flat as a soufflé
at a polka contest.
Who will test us
with a toothpick?

We're raw in the middle, Sylvia,
no matter how we're sliced.

Overbeaten to stiff peaks
the texture of mud pies,
yet burned on the outside to a
fine golden crisp.

Beauty Queen Never

I'm in a beauty
pageant and have made
it to the questions round.
The Vaseline on my teeth helps
me smile despite my dry mouth.
The lights above are blinding.
If this part of the contest doesn't
end soon, my bouffant
hair will fall flat.
I remember to
keep my ankles crossed,
but this hot pink sequined evening
gown itches. Most of my concentration
is on not scratching delicate places on
national TV. Thank God my
false eyelashes are
staying put. The
twiggy girl next to
me has quit talking,
followed by applause. The MC
turns to me and says, "Miss Kansas,
blah blah blah blah, blah blah blah.
What would you do?" Glossed smile
frozen, I smile bigger and say,
"Well, I would do anything in
this situation that promotes
world peace." Inside I'm
thinking, almost loud
enough to be heard,
the first thing I am
doing when I get
off this stage is
losing this damn
pair of panty hose.

9/11

The room behind them is on fire.
They stand at the open window,
silhouetted by smoke and burning jet fuel,
a man, a woman.
One decision: burn or fly.

Are they work spouses toiling together?
Until today.
They turn to face each other,
decide,
grab hands and step out.

Is it an instant,
wind roaring in their ears,
or a lifetime before impact as they
free fall from Hell to wake
in Heaven?

Hymn for Gen X and Millennials

This is what it feels like to have
no place, no chair, no standing room,
not even space enough to
expand your lungs.

There are 20,000 people crammed beside you,
in front, behind.
Could standing bodies be stacked,
someone would find a way.

The Baby Boom American Dream
is our nightmare.
We stand in bread lines for
bread and wine we will never taste,
born too late to claim a portion or
be handed crumbs from pitying strangers.

Our dreams are barren with no fields
in which to grow them.
Our futures fallow without children,
homes, or cars to drive away.
Fields and fuel belong to those preceding us.

We would work harder were there room.

Instead, we starve immobilized
like cattle for slaughter
while bloated Boomers chant,
"Make America Great Again"
as they march to church.

What would Jesus do?

Crammed together we will never know,
will never see beyond a sea of bodies
Christ's second coming.

In the Town of Knife

In the town of Knife there are no shortcuts.
Earning one's keep slashes through muscle, sinew,
scrapes against sound bones.
We water our lawns with blood;
the weeds flourish.
Everyone lives on the edge in Knife.

I'm not the sharpest blade in the block,
but even I get this point.
Life is pointless in Knife or anywhere else.
The weeds remind me when I crawl home,
saw at their stems with a dull edge.

None of us are proud of our scabs, nicks, or gashes.
Scars straight, jagged, mean nothing.
Bright seams or fading stripes of flesh,
those are mere freckles in Knife.
Scattered across our hides,
they depict constellations of choices
we've had to make to live here.

We eat while bleeding.
Pay rent with stitches or starve
with pristine flesh.
The choice is always
ours. That finally
is the only
point in Knife
and still we
choose
it.

Blue Collar Saint

Most days I perform miracles.
I get out of bed.
I force myself to don clothes,
go to work.

Then on assembly lines
I fit pieces together,
box them fast as I can
though I can't keep up.

If I am truly gifted,
I remember not to cry.
And if I am extraordinary,
sometimes I smile.

My brain is broken
so mis-wired it shoots
impulses in delicate parts of
itself far from intended receptors.

Despite these burned injuries
I continue to build parts,
to speak and stand.

I go home
a garden of pain blooming
throughout my body,
throughout my heart,
joints and tendons pulsing.

I fall into bed,
dream of fishing in flood waters,
of finding family treasures

in newly appearing rooms
of the house.

Then I rise like Lazarus,
repeat the thaumaturgy,
and return to work.

I greet other saints at the door.
We nod and brush haloes.
We are essential and meaningless
as we build parts for management
yet remain standing,
miracle workers too weak to
change water into wine.

Flight or Fight

A TSA worker swan dives from a balcony
suspended in time, in motion,
until his weight destroys an atrium.
His colleagues are left to corral the
herd of frequent flyers, business class, vacationers
and their children away from the devastation
before hysteria can ensue stampede.
Stunned yet standing, travelers enter
alternate gates, board departing flights,
perhaps some cry.
Eventually everyone heads home.

A factory employee arrives to work, surprise in a lunch pail.
Before last break, his pistol punctuates
office conversations, and the wounded
still ambulatory break like quail,
a starburst of opposing directions.
The shooter returns to the floor and
directs his laser at lines of fleeing people
he has toiled beside for years.
Bullets follow green beams as bodies
dodge to doors or fall in growing spills of blood.
Some aren't going home.

Covid-19 2020

For the first time in my life
I am essential.
It only took a pandemic

and auto accessories:
squeegees,
extended wash brushes,

funnels for fluids, and
snow brooms.
I am integral for inventory.

Thank God. I was beginning
to think
I was nothing.

Changelings

Zilpha Keatley Snyder taught me about grief,
not fitting in with my peers or my family,
that it was painful to lose your only friend,
and how being odd in an even world
was a hollow ache of shed and unshed tears.

But her pages pliéd music my heart
hummed, haunting minor and solitary.
Being different wasn't criminal or faux pas,
she said, your outside was not you,
and your true self was magic.

I could be a fairy princess dancing in
trees, balanced amid limbs and branches,
a diadem of flowers and tiny wings.
I could project the possibility of
grace if I acted graceful,
even if only by myself.
I could be beautiful as the
flowers I pretended to gather.

It didn't matter if I really was a goblin
exchanged for a mortal child.
Inside I was the Milky Way and petals,
birthing stars and prisms of light
as I fought to place my feet
on human roads and still be fae.

To Kate Spade

The thing about handbags is you
put all your stuff in them
and tote it around.

There is a handle and room
for lipstick, keys, compact,
tampons,
decree of separation.

You've got the whole world in your handbag.
Your shit is together.

Scarves are flighty, flippy-floppy
accents waving Hello, Look at me, SOS.
They slip through your fingers,
puddle on the floor.

Noose-like serpents of silk or rayon.
Why rope them near your throat,
the energetic chakra of communication?
Your Voice?

Knot that fabric somewhere else
or weave rugs soft enough to
float beneath your feet.

Grip a handle of some handbag prismatic,
throw that strap across your shoulder.
Jangle those contents with the sway
of hips and arm swings.
Sing your presence until windows in
every building shatter.

II.
Praise the Lord and Pass the Medication

Amitriptyline

Sounds like something one would jump on
or an antidote given Superman
for kryptonite poisoning.

Maybe a newly discovered mineral
that improves the eyesight
when taken twice a day,

or the Princess Amitriptyline shot by
Bolsheviks in a basement, then lost
as the stone of a ring.

Perhaps cheap fuel for compact cars
or a mountain on Atlantis
poking through the sea.

The sea nymph, Amitriptyline, doomed
by prophecy to marry one
her son will best.

Or the newest thing in washers
guaranteed for life or 30,000
spins, whichever's first.

Amitriptyline, a line of eye paint,
hair dyes, and lip gloss because
you're not worth it.

Abilify

Abilify is my alibi.
It makes me not give an F Y.
I don't even give an F U,
and isn't that what antidepressants
are supposed to do?

In emotional stasis until I die
as long as I take Abilify.

Wellbutrin

Round tablet
a circle
complete
whole

Tired Yellow or
Pale Blue
dose
depending

Easy to swallow

Embossed numbers
and name brand
upside down
form a smiley face

Why then am
I not
smiling?

Cymbalta

Cymbalta is a waltz in an empty room,
numb feet and a piano out of tune.
And you wonder what you take it for,
a solitary dance on a dusty floor?

The things we do to forgo pain,
take pills to make things right again,
as if a dose
would bring relief
and wellness like an earned reprieve.

That is the lie
Cymbalta tells.
The dance is false, steps full of stealth,
each day lone dips and sway, no lasting mental health.

Reckless Driving

Before my gallbladder was removed
I had dreams of near collision,
careening around corners on no wheels,
red and blue lights in the rearview mirror.
I could feel paper of a citation between my fingers
though when I awoke there was nothing.

I said to myself, "I'll be careful on the road."
I didn't know my tires were spinning
on self-made gravel.

But I've come straight out of this fishtail.
I stay in my lane, obey the speed limit,
read all the signs,
even those inside the car.

I Was Here

My life falls and breaks as
glass in splinters, chips, particled
dust, and I should leave it be,
but the ruins won't let me alone.
So I trace my fingers
through the twisted shatters.
Their tips are cut on points that
matter to no one but myself,
and I write my name in glass,
in blood.

Brenda Leigh White

Escape Artist

The window stood open; all I had to do was jump.

Too bad it was the first floor.
Now I'm tangled in a rose bush of regrets,
curtains hanging out the window
waving goodbye.

My sprained ankle and the
rose thorns remind me I'm still here.
It's all about extrication,
unsnarling one stickered branch
after another, and limping
to the welcome mat,
key underneath.

Inside, I can close the door,
window, and curtains,
pop open Neosporin,
slather my wounds.

Maybe all I needed
was a little Lidocaine.

Solar-Powered

Despite grey sky
my solar-powered Cupid
swings his arms left to right

Such tiny bits of light
minuscule sparks
and Cupid does a joyful dance

Could we have the chance
to winnow light from dark
gather rays like grain

Dance despite pain
and harvest hope
It takes so little light

Cupid swinging left to right
shows the way
heartbeat rocking on a single ray

Catnapping

The cat insists I must recline,
provide ample room for her repose
several times a day.
I'm an overstuffed sofa at best,
lumps, bumps, jiggles.
Her only complaint is kneading
her paws to soften and readjust
my landscape to her leisure,
smooth wrinkles in my clothing
with her claw tips.

I should protest her ministrations,
but vibrating contentment from
her throat and chest,
she lulls me in sleepy compliance.
I am the cat's slave, her daybed,
the launchpad for her dreamscapes
and my own.

My Favorite Pair of Shoes

My holographic silver Birkenstocks
have walked miles in Eureka Springs
on Mud Street, Pearl, and Spring.

They balanced my weight as I studied
Luna moths above my head in
the stairwells of the Best Western motel.
They reposed on a glittery red buggy's
floorboard as I rode in a parade
high in the backseat gripping a roll bar.

Up serpentine roads lined with
crowds and eccentric or antique houses,
my Birkenstocks cradled my feet,
iridescent loops embracing both big toes.

They led me to a Tarot reader at the
back of a magnetic energy bracelet shop,
my shoes bright as auras.
To fudge-works and hot pepper products,
antiques, and King Magnus, the snow Bengal cat.
Each step was magic, dreamlike,
strolling through that enchanted place
in my prismatic shoes.

Mended

My shoulders have been
stitched together like a
ragdoll's, white scar
seams on left and right

as if some child
swung me 'round
by my arms and
tendons gave with
loosened threads.

Tacked together
blue fish line fiber,
a surgeon's
made me whole.

Now I am ready to
spin, dance, or be
flopped beneath a tree
forgotten until
morning.

God Makes Mistakes

They walk on two legs
and look like everyone else,
but their broken edges
catch on other people
leaving them bleeding,
sometimes scarred.

Mistakes can't help
their nature.
Their souls are thorns
and weeds
if they have souls.

Sometimes Mistakes are
black holes that
pull marrow, joy,
hope from people in
close proximity.
God made Mistakes
so empty.

He forgot to attach
warning labels
"Caution: contact with this
substance is life-threatening."
Back away from God's mistakes.
Save yourselves.

Gay

We were friends who finished each other's shenanigans,
voice-synched deviant dialogue to black-and-white films.
Now your much slender face wears a beard,
and your white uniform seems as antiseptic as the hospital in
    which we stand.
Facing each other in an elevator, our backs against opposing walls,
    your face is pensive.
"I need to tell you something important now. Okay?"
I'm not dressed for ceremony in jeans and hooded jacket.
"Okay," and I wish I understood your reticence.
My father's trip to St. Luke's has left me sloth-like,
unable to reach for branches, to interpret my own language, to
    breathe.
You pause, pondering a pronouncement once private,
"I'm gay." It falls scentless and without hue to the floor of the
    rising elevator.
I'm light as the seed of a dandelion—so that's all.
"That doesn't bother you?" I tell you, "No."
As you bury me in your embrace, I feel you never knew me, gay,
    straight, or whatever.

Leznupar

My hair is falling out, each day by the fistful,
in my comb, in the tub drain.
I let go of it above the waste basket and
observe its tangled descent.

I'm not on chemo, no life threatening illness,
except depression. I'm just fat,
short of oxygen and energy,
my scalp gleaming through.

My new age books say hair is creativity.
I've kept mine long for years,
relished its crowned glory,
side-parted the straight lanks.

The only benefit of being female,
I thought, was keeping my hair.

As I sweep up the sheddings,
scrape nests from the drains,
I'm puzzled by my erosion.

I long for the time
when my only concern was
grey.

Bound for Extinction

I am a dinosaur
stomping through the maze of love.
Brain walnut-sized,
feet like shovel scoops,
I have no handle on this game.
Every turn dead-ends me,
and I don't want to play.

How did I walk into this puzzle?

Yet here I am,
my steps slower than a heartbeat,
lumbering toward a center
more massive than a meteor's mark,
and still I cannot find it.

Note Left on the Kitchen Table for my Family

Dear Ones,

Have gone to Hell as you
asked me to so often.
On the road of Good Intentions
with unfortunate outcomes,
the way should be
clear as six-lane freeways
but hopefully not as crowded.

Does this multitude of travelers intend
good or crumbs of kindness
to anyone?
Just we miserable meek
inflicting unintentional
wounds as we
crawl on the earth
we are bequeathed.

I would take a handbasket, but
alas, my ass is too wide,
and I can't fathom
travel in such a contraption.
Were you here,
I'm sure you could advise.

As to my return,
I cannot say.
Having never gone to this location,
I am uncertain of time involved,
best mode of travel, or
possibility of return at all.
Will do my absolute best.

Love to you all despite
my intentions.

                Me

III.
Marked on God's Atomic Map

Turkeys Traverse Timber

Turkeys traverse timber
clucking like flocks of chickens,
pecking, scratching through fallen leaves
for bugs and plant shoots,
their pace a Sunday stroll.

A spy behind trees and brush
would know this,
domesticated language
from wild birds.

In the spatter of a spring storm,
they cross clearings as if
coyotes and bobcats
or even spies did not exist.
Hawks could be on other continents,
owls on the moon.

And a spy would learn amid raindrops,
how thunder reverberates in one's chest,
even a gentle kind,
how Toms conversing the ordinary
suddenly gobble three and four syllable
curses in response to each of
Heaven's grumbles.

Controlled Burn

Fire smolders across my inner landscape.
With all the brush, dried weeds, and dead debris
the full acreage should ignite,
blacken from field to field until the
detritus is a memory drawn in ash.

I don't mean to hold the gas and matches,
to make the flames so stationary
I am burned from the inside out.
Fire by its nature is a traveler
devouring grass, wood, leaves, and flesh alike.

There must be some trick to clearing land,
driving fire forward so a herd of flames
consumes the trash that prevents new growth.
Even something wild needs direction.

I just want to plant my heart in a
greening pasture,
stretch its tendrils to the sky amid new grass
and wave in the wind and
sunlight.

After the Service

He never bothered to tell us
she passed and was buried
in the country cemetery,
watched over by God,
mocking birds, meadowlarks,
prairie wind to lull her sleep.

We found out at another funeral.

Service end, we drifted to
family stones, lichen-covered
marble veined as varicose,
stark as a knife blade.
History and memory numbed
us to the cold.

Goodbye is a hollow word
when unanswered,
but we huddled by the most recent stone,
wept together with twenty-year-old grief,
the only goodbye we could muster.
Wind whipping around us
mourned as well.

He approached to speak
face bright with greeting and
stumbled into our heartbreak
which widened his eyes,
closed his lips.
Then he jerked his arm
to the south
"She's buried over there,"
and turned to leave.

Teardrops coating our eyelashes,
we smiled at each other, and eventually,
ambled south.

Family Photo

It's easy to spot me,
out of focus,
off to one side.
My eyes blur
away from lens
and family.
I could be a developmental mar,
some flaw in the negative.

Everyone else is smiling
or squinting,
shoulders braced for
the photographer.
They know when to say cheese,
when to stand perfectly still.

I try my best
until my nose itches
or some fly sends my arms
wind milling precisely
as the shutter clicks.

I'm some many-layered mirage,
a mist of human atoms.

Someone should teach me how to pose,
how to stare at the camera
and smile without
trembling.

Hackberry Emperors

Hackberry Emperors hold court
in flight around the trees.
We sit or stand in shade
drinking Sprite, Dr. Pepper,
Mountain Dew.
Our conversation drifts
in and out with the breezes
when an Emperor drops to
rest on my shoulder
unspiraling its tongue.
It pokes my shirt for nectar
that isn't there.
I still myself for miracles,
marvel that a butterfly
 would deign to find me sweet.

Then another Emperor lights on
the rim of someone's can
unfurls its coil for a stolen
sip of Sprite.

Inspired, I fill a bottle cap,
offer ambrosia to my guest
who tentatively taps the surface
sucks the carbonated sugar
serious as stone.

Soon, a sprinkling of Emperors
descend and dine
from this can rim
that bottle mouth or cap
until everyone of us has dispensed
drink for this kaleidoscope of kings.

My Toad

My toad disappeared.
Has she run away from home?
Gotten a job in town?
Joined the circus or hopped on
a midnight train to Georgia?

Perhaps she entered
Witness Protection and changed
her name to Lily?
Or abducted by aliens,
she has peed on their digits.

Has my toad been caught
and eaten by a serpent?
Has she joined a cult
selling flowers for their youth
group to travel to Korea?

Does she owe someone
money and fled collectors?
Joined the armed service
or a ballet troupe dancing
in the chorus of Swan Lake?

Maybe she simply
ran away with gypsies and
predicts futures or fortunes
in a satin tent sitting
sagely before a crystal ball.

Hearts Are the Most Useless Things

Hearts are the most useless things.
Third wings on flightless birds,
pebbles dropped into wells without splash.
They lead us into tribulations
barefoot across lava flows.
The only things burning
are hands grasping for
other hands but catching
air.

Still
the heart sees an Everest and says
at the top we will belong
to God, a crevasse, a cloud,
other climbers,
surely a
Sherpa . . .

Alone and caged in ribs
the heart starves to death,
awaiting seeds, crumbs,
the murmur of some hope
drowned out by
silence.

Going Home

When we made the last turn west
on Diamond Creek Road,
the glimpse of stone house roof
from high places in the road
filled my heart with such hope.

Heaven was attainable in a car ride
despite the twists and turns or
inclines and descents of gravel.
The roof through tree limbs meant
we would soon turn into a circling lane.
My grandparents would greet us
with smiles, embraces, or pats on the back.

Every heavy pebble weighted in my heart,
all accoutrements of city dwelling,
dropped through me and dissipated
into the dirt and limestone layers
beneath my feet.

For an instant I could love and be loved
without flinching, without tears,
finally belonging to a place and persons,
as close to being home as
I ever could be.

Recalling Grandma in the West Timber

I think sometimes the wood and fields are you,
greens of grapevine, willow, and cress,
heart full of undulating creek riffle and crow calls,
breeze through brush like exhalations.
Even deer and haunting bluebirds invoke you where I walk,
at the sycamore tree one person cannot embrace,
at the swimming hole where I tore my shirt on thorns.
I wish you truly present, palpable
as the snake I step over or the shadowing hawk above.
Heavens knows you could be here; how would I know?
With Lewis, your brother, astride a pair of phantom ponies,
but I smell the fresh-turned field, see only spring azures
thick as raindrops amid the greening timber.
How so many can navigate such a tiny spot
or did you bring them here to show me your hello?

September

Summer slips through my fingers
yellow and green leaves spiraling down.
Sunflowers and asters have
replaced the roses and tomatoes.
The blue, blue sky is just a tease
with the last of the cumulous.

We've taken down the pool,
gallons seeping into the lawn.
It's time to place fresh hay or
straw in the dog houses,
to think of carrying plants inside.
Cirrus mare's tails sweep the sky.

Sunset arrives earlier each night,
reminds us Earth needs rest,
but like an infant fighting sleep,
I fuss at balmy days and cooler
nights, golden leaves, tawny grass.

September says light and dark
are equal now but I see darkness
lengthen and say, "Oh, no."
I long for thunderstorms, for the
melted butter warmth of summer days,
for butterflies and fragrant blossoms.
Turning leaves and blonded grass mean
autumn is just winter's precursor,
and I am discontent.

Seagulls in Kansas

Seagulls have flown inland,
brash white against the blue sky.
What are they doing here on the plains
that are no longer a Bahaman sea?
That was millions of years ago.
Now the waters are native grass and cedar
and hedge.

Are the gulls on vacation?
Tired of endless blues and greens
stretching one horizon to another,
of roiling waves and waterspouts?
Longing for salt of the earth
instead of salt water?

This is the place then to snatch
soybeans spilled in dirt,
gorge on grains in fields
instead of fish and garbage
near a shore.
This is the place to circle
wide in an endless sky,
sparkling pristine as tiny bits of
glass refracting light from a
setting sun.

Brenda Leigh White

Fall Memory

At dusk in the timber
I head back to the house
with the black cat
who followed me to the creek.

There are coyotes and owls
I don't see so I look back,
make sure he is close,
that we both return home.

Sunlight dips the skyline,
darkens timber, and
scratching sounds nearby make me
jerk on the well-worn path,

but it is only a possum
climbing between trees
who freezes when our eyes connect,
his smile revealing pointed teeth.

"Come on," I call to the cat
barely visible in the dark
who meows and scampers up.
The house is still some distance.

Then movement draws my sight.
Behind us, the black silhouette of an owl,
wingspan nearly wide as the creek,
glides above the water in silence
and floats away from us.

Unintended

The planets aren't in retrograde anymore.
Even so, this morning I've managed to crush
three snails in two different yards.

Minding their own business on concrete and
soft grass, they had no way of knowing their
slow treks would end under my big feet.

So much for a peaceful breakfast
under a grapevine trellis, in the mint
patch, or munching a leaf on the patio,

all interrupted by unwitting destruction
brought by a snail-loving idiot who
hadn't the sense to look down first.

And why not look down with rain
the night before, an obvious portend of
snails venturing from seclusion and safety?

Yet the crunch of their tiny homes and lives
will stay with me for days, another set of
cracks in a heart broken but not apart.

I ended the lives of innocents, unintentionally or
not. Who knows what other devastations
I have wrought?

Tiny Miracles

I've held a baby bluebird
in my hands, steel grey feathers,
an unconscious gold finch,
a cardinal chick with broken leg,
a crow.

I've held an infant
western box turtle,
a coral ring-necked snake,
a corn snake, a baby bull snake,
a blue tongued skink,
an uncountable number of toads,
nickel-size to palm full.

My hands have cradled
baby squirrels,
wild baby cottontails,
some so young they were furless,
small mice.

I've cupped baby bullheads
not one half inch long,
minnows, cricket frogs,
crawfish.

I've marveled at the shape
movement and heartbeats
of everything wild I have held—
their fine fur or feathers,
slick dry scales,
soft wet flesh,
each a tiny miracle in
my hands.

Simultaneously,
I am smaller than an atom,
bigger than the sky.

Oriole

I'm looking through a smudge on our glass door
and hear the oriole outside.

Spring is never present until the oriole arrives,
song sparkling high in the trees
more orange than he is,
neon even.

My heart wants to soar in
his elevation so I go outside,
scour the elm's topmost boughs
for his dayglow flash.

Such a marvel that he melds
his sips of air into trills clear as water,
sounds that splash like droplets of
gold on violets and new grass.

I long to replicate his music
but whistle brass imitations.
Perhaps it is enough.
My off pitch tones call for his correction.

He lights nearby, repeats his melody,
and I whistle back triangulating
his location by response.
Who knows what we are singing.
With any foreign language
we learn the curse words first.
I could be telling him his parents
never married.
He could be calling me an ugly horse's ass.

I don't care as long as he keeps
trilling and remains in sight.
I'm tiny beneath the treetop,
but my heart blossoms like a
newborn star.

Conversing with something wild,
receiving his response,
I and the oriole are
marked on God's atomic map.

Strange as I am, I ponder other humans,
people who are so lonely
behind smudged glass
they can't call to an oriole.

IV.
Thirty Day Chip

Far Side Love at World's End

Arlene dons her favorite
A-line dress and pearls the
size of Bing cherries
for her blind date at the
Rainbow's End Saloon.

She plans to take her best friend,
Sylvia, to meet an astrophysicist
and his used car salesman brother.

Arlene will know her date
by the meat-eating orchid on his lapel
and his copy of *A Brief History of Time*
tucked under his left arm.

They will rhumba, samba, and tango
'til the cows go home to Farmer Brown,
and they will mistake the stars in their eyes for
Love Everlasting, neither recognizing
reflective glints of a mushroom cloud
blooming in the dawn.

To the Moon

I would never eat dryer lint.
I would never wear tinfoil bloomers.
I would never buy a cruise on a UFO.
I would never do the hokey pokey naked.
I would never go to the moon and look for Alice Cramdon.
I would always like to think Ralph never meant it.
And I promise I will never send care packages to Uranus.

Spaghetti Supper Tango

He offers to make supper

extends his hand for the
package of spaghetti
she smacks across his palm.

He rips open the box with his teeth,
sets it on a stack of dry goods
near the pantry shelves.

Now for sauce.

He flings cabinet doors wide,
rummages for Traditional,
paces before the shelves.
There is only Meat sauce.
Wooden spoon between his teeth,
he stomps.
This will not suffice.

She counters, "Why not?"
and turns her face aside.
His head snaps negative.
Traditional is penultimate.

On her knees before the shelving
she digs—past canned corn,
diced tomatoes, pumpkin, and sliced pears.

Meat sauce and nothing more.

Rising, with the Meat sauce can,
she elbows the open

spaghetti by accident.
It scatters across the floor,
blond strings
crunching beneath their feet.
She kicks her shoe at the mess,
thumps Meat sauce on the table.

Words and hand gestures
staccato the kitchen.
He spins, departs, and slams the door.

Circling her toe on linoleum
she dips for her purse.
Her adagio is a trip to the store,
a return home by herself
with Traditional sauce.

Blank When it Comes to Verse

I would love to compose a poem in iambic pentameter.
However, so far it exceeds my poetic parameter.
There's something off-kilter about writing lines with five feet.
Unlike the Go-Gos, I can't sing, "We've got the beat."
Frost and Shakespeare, Marlowe and so many others
have written great lines of five feet with such ease, those old
    mothers.
Why can't I produce five feet lines in some sonnets like them?
After all, they could do it and they were quite woefully men.

Maybe my milieu is solely four beats and no more?
Limericks, ballads, and quatrains are all I can write
Like seasons, leap years, compass points, and the elements all.
Even a square and its corners are naturally four.
So in posterity I and my works will alight
with four metered verses all fit for a bathroom stall.

"To the People Who Lost One Shoe on the Side of the Highway" Facebook Meme

My empathetic nature causes me to inquire
what happened to you to leave one shoe
on a highway shoulder?
Curiosity fills in the blanks:

>Fleeing the chainsaw massacrist on your bicycle
>you shed your shoe in haste.
>
>Hanging your feet out a car window
>one shoe untied and—whoosh
>it is gone.
>
>Observing a police car, you remember,
>Oh shit, your stash is in your shoe.
>
>Your soon-to-be ex-girlfriend throws your
>open suitcase and then you out of the hybrid.
>Scooping up your belongings when a semi offers you a ride,
>you miss your shoe.
>
>You open a brand new shoebox and
>as a philanthropic amputee,
>you cast out of the car window one shoe
>in hopes a mirror image amputee
>finds providence in the discard.
>
>Tripping on LSD, you find your clothes on fire.
>You strip the flaming garments off and
>out the window, amid your screaming,
>flies one shoe.
>
>Your husband confesses he is leaving you
>for his girlfriend and their baby.

With no revolver handy, you fling at his
two-timing head the only weapon available,
a single athletic sneaker.

While you mutter over a flat tire,
some random serial killer bashes your head
with a tire iron and drags you to his trunk.
All that marks your disaster
is a shoe.

Hitching rides at midnight, you are abducted by the Greys.
Frozen in their tractor beam,
you rise to your anal probe while your
shoe plops back to Terra Firma.

Despite any scenario in which you
sacrifice one shoe to public roadways,
I can't help but worry about your outcome.
As you hop on one foot to the shoe store,
May you keep your balance,
your mind, knees, and elbows all unscathed.
I pray your shoelace retains its bow.
May your size be in abundance
in colors you prefer,
your cash be plentiful,
your coupons unexpired.

And for all that is holy,
Please keep this pair together.
A million of us or more
would like you off our minds.

Haiku

Who knew Florida's
frost would drop iguanas from
trees like ripened fruit

Snow moon rising
flames orange amid the stars
a disc on fire

Snowflakes descend in
their airy waltz to earth and
rest on silent ground

Winter grasps April
in claws of cold wind and ice
squelching dreams of spring

Watercress returns
to a spring's stream clear water
seeping through limestone

A blue hairstreak
rests in wild plum blossoms
the first butterfly

Blue herons nest
in sycamores so high their
cradles scrape Heaven

February 2, 2020

The diner's breakfast special is
sausage in multiple forms:
patties, links, Polish,
kielbasa, and gravy over biscuits.

Twelve hours later I realize it's
Ground Hog.

It is his day,
and he's seen his shadow
on this date that is a
mirror of itself.

Spring will soon arrive,
provided we aren't entangled in
a loop of time repeating the same
twenty four hours until we get
our Karma right.

As if February wasn't long
enough already,
twenty eight days lingering
like one hundred.

Let us leap into March then,
spring forward from the
infinite date.
The year is waving
from February's far side
Come,
the rest of your life awaits.

Mardi Gras 2020

Fat Tuesday
and my life is leaner
than a starved man.
What can I give up for Lent?
My hunger?
An empty plate?
A rib and two fleshless knuckles?

Everyone else is at the party
flinging beads and alcoholic shots.
They GET Carnival,
even in masks and feathers
of every hue.

I'm just removed and
rendered joyless.
Perhaps I'm too sober,
music and laughter so raucous.

I can give up Hope for Lent,
my tribal membership,
tenuous at best.
I can give up counting my
disappointments by twos.

Waking on Wednesday,
my picture should appear on milk cartons.
Instead, I am draped across a bed,
corpse-like,
attempting prayer with a
mouth full of ashes.

Memorial Day 2019

Mulready's is closed.
Deb and I forgot to confer with
Facebook for the info so
we sit on the bench outside,
notebooks in our laps,
my pen scritching paper,
her keys popping,
awaiting predicted rain.

We could press our faces to glass,
"Let us in! Let us in!"
But I don't want Mulready's hours
imprinted on my forehead.
Deb is fine with two of us
instead of twelve as long as
there's a face to catch her phrasing.

We compose a poem:
what foolishness feels like,
how it looks like two people
sitting outside a closed bar,
how it smells of impending rain.

Our souls glow so fiercely
we are warm as we write.
Our incandescence melds.
We sit on the bench
And illuminate the darkened street
for miles.

Monday Evening at Writers' Group

"Hi.
My name is Brenda, and
I am an overthinking, neurotic,
emotionally damaged introvert.
With depression."

"Hi, Brenda," everyone smiles and waves.

"It's been one week, four days, eight hours,
and thirty-five minutes
since my last meltdown."

The room applauds.
"I know, right? Eighteen days
and I get a pen."

"This week has been rough,
breathing, breathing all the time,
but I kept going.
Not a whimper.
I really want that pen.

Then the tricky part,
I had to get out of bed."

People nod their heads.

"Blank pages appear out of nowhere
every single day,
Dementors sucking my energy.
They drift from the walls,
float about the room,
flash themselves in my face.

Brenda Leigh White

Then the inner critic shows up
and unpacks all of her
baggage, that bitch.
You think she could
call first.
Leaves her nylons and
underwear hanging in the bathroom.
Follows me around,
breathing down my neck.

Still, I sat down at the table,
not one tear.
I didn't sigh or gasp.

I finally managed to
pick up a pencil and
scribbled a few lines.

Yes, it's messy, though legible.
The page was stabbed
a few times,
torn and smudged,
but I left words and images.
Words and Images.
Who knows?
I may try for a
metaphor next time.

Anyway,
that's my week.
And no meltdowns.
I'm working toward
that six-month notebook."

Everyone applauds.
Some wipe their eyes.
"Way to go."
"You can do this."
Their smiles brighten the bar.

Curtis steps up,
"Thank you for sharing, Brenda.
Keep up the good work.
We all know how hard this can be.

Who wants to go next?"

Breaking Writer's Block

An ice pick would be tedious
chipping words, half-thoughts, letters,
eons without slightest indentation.

A chisel then, hardly better.
Mounds of detritus and broken fonts,
disintegrating ideas,
a wall barely scraped.

Perhaps a plasma cutter—
surgical, but excising meat
as well as meaningless
doubts and worries crystalized by
time's reiteration, cauterized
clean and lifeless.
Images, the shining phrase
scattered amid litter.

A jackhammer—
too jarring, creating
more injury than inroads
brain bounced against the skull
paragraphs, pages, columns
ripped aside.

What to do with
this Chinese wall?

Better then, to bury it,
kick grass across the top,
trot away
whistling.

Dear Autocorrect,

What the fork? I'm so tired
of your shirt. How can I
send concise massages to my
fiends if you continually change
my weirds?

Please cease and detest
connecting my languid.
Use the words I chews.

Think you very much,

Me

Tuffy on Sunday Morning

I stitched closed
the cat's "baby"
her favorite amputee
mouse
Innards reinserted
flesh pulled taut
and sides laced
tight with quilting
thread, the "baby"
lives again

This morning
she carried
her precious into
the kitchen calling
around its bulk
the song queens
sing to kittens
when teaching them
to hunt

She has no kittens
but her mouth
and heart are full
It is Sunday
and resurrection
enough for
her

Tempests and Teacups

It's been raining in the attic for a week,
water pooling on the floor.
Strobes of lightning periodically
outline the attic door.
It's not leaking in from outside.

Could it cause a fire?

Most disturbing, thunder upstairs
rattles dishes in the kitchen.
We teeter around pots and
bowls littering the
kitchen floor as we still
cups in cabinets,
our fingers like prunes.

We can't have anyone over.
How do you explain a tempest
inside a house? Floorboards groaning
above your head, the smell of
ozone in the parlor.
Blankets in the guest room
dense with rain.

So we ride out the lightning,
rumbling, and showers,
mopping floors and wringing
out curtains.
I think we should move
before the china breaks.

Fools and Money

"Money is fire," she tells me, "a trailing
finger on a curve of the moon
that slides off the surface
into silence, into space."

Having felt those heads of presidents
heat my fingertips and pockets,
burn my lips when kissed goodbye,
I nod, "yes."

My coffers empty like a black hole.
My head is vacant, silent as a
moon with pock marks and canyons
coalescing into a goofy face.

Money seems more remote
than the curve of Halley's Comet,
the neighboring nebulae, or stars that glimmer
like new pennies twice hot.

"You can sing sparks down," she says,
"The moon hears supplications and
will send your fingers fire,
showering pelts of gold."

Leaning back, she stares toward
Saturn, inhales and slowly sighs,
"The trick is not to flinch."

Tenacity

Grandma B married 16 times before she found her one.
She filled an empty well with alcoholics,
with vows God joined and life put asunder,
with disappearing for weeks on end to be found
knocked prone by destitution and prostitution
thousands of miles from home.
She looked for love, for connection, in all places,
savory, sour, sweet.

Something made her dust off her heart,
her hope, and rise like Lazarus to try on Living
again and again no matter what it cost,
how badly it fit, or ripped apart.

She was no quitter.
And she managed to glean a forty year marriage
from the dross of her life lessons, each one
hard as creek gravel on bare feet.
She still believed she could share God's ear,
convince Him to save a premature child
solely with love she poured from her heart
like syrup and melted butter on pancakes
she prepared by herself.

God was in the details and disasters.
Faith was a matter of patience spread over years
as she crawled from her knees each time to stand.

v.
Stardust

Palmystery

I hold out my hand
without heart
line or head line
Instead the line is simian

I am a law unto
myself with heart
and head ruled
equally
One is not
above Or
below

I am *And* amid a
world of *Or*—
    reason or emotion
    mind or body
    succeed or fail

I succeed and fail
reason through emotions
My body speaks
this to the mind
in lines I can't
ignore
grooves of equal
length and depth
across both
palms

So what is the
future for *And*
amid *Or*

My fate line
is so straight
but for its cracks
and breaks

Prayer to My Angels

Can you bathe my heart in a
basin of tepid water,
rinse the road wear and grime
encapsulating the desiccated
muscle until the mud shells away
in thickened curls?

I want to feel light again,
a soap bubble floating across fields
of broom and clover.
I want to hover in treetops,
pretend flight is possible,
that dreams are the multi-colored
wings I flex and steer skyward.

Let me know relief a traveler feels
when calloused soles are soothed
in clear water, briefly
unencumbered by the road.

If You Believe in ME—Let Go

I have let go the branch,
falling,
endlessly
falling.

If not for the loss of altitude,
my mind could compose a
shopping list:
        Fabric softener
        New shoes
        Cat litter
        Dish soap.

But altitude is everything.

The whoosh of gravity deafens me,
loose hair whipping eyes and face.
I cannot see a landing space
through the blur of tears.

Will this end with a bang
or a thud?
Or a cradling catch in
His hands?

Is Faith merely this:
my body the broken gate
I pass through
from this World to the
New?

Indifference

God ignores me,
so many of us,
(at least in that
I'm not alone).
I understand.
There are multitudes
to think about.
Thank Him, Jesus loves me,
but look what God
did to Him?
The one He held
most dear.

Afternoon Visit

My Guardian Angel dropped in for tea,
alighted in silence illuminating the door's silhouette.
I saw the incandescent glow before she rang the bell.
Embarrassed, I had to wash a cup
then put the kettle on, search for tea and honey.

Normally, surprises spill me sideways.
Her appearance out of blue was less than breath,
and I'm learning not to question grace.
I simply pulled out a chair, swept crumbs aside,
set down the shining cup.

She chose chamomile with rose hips and
let my cat settle in her lap,
make biscuits on the iridescent fabric of her robe.
Sometimes salvation comes in quiet,
low as a cat's purr.
Healing is easy as herb tea and
basking in the auras of angels.

Lost in Translation

Someday my Guardian Angel
will forget himself,
feel his thoughts into
the soup of atoms
I call, "I,"
and explain his crippled hand.

The sinister puzzle
he cups beneath heart and lungs
rests atop his emotional chakra,
its fingers so twisted
he cannot point me
any direction
but inward.

Which way is right?

Feelings are a language
I can't read.
Their pictures send me
half the story.

My heart is a vessel
too chipped, too broken
to embrace my own emotions,
too porous to hold a clue.

Which feelings are mine leaking out?
Which some other's bleeding in?

All my Angel would have to do
is speak,

not in tongues,
not in tones,
and not in emotional vibrations
that make no sense
to me.

Doll Dreams and Handmade Wishes

Iris Tallulah Bliss
wishes on straight pins
and marking pencils.
She got the point at birth,
stitched seams, curves clipped,
and swell of cheek packed tight with fleece.

God is a mess of fingers and thimble,
a large face cooing,
"You're cute," who plops one on a chair.

Pins hold things true
and markers save face.
For Iris, this is Grace
pristine as tiny buttons or
eyelashes secured one thread
at a time.

Wishes are clever as coordinating cottons,
practical as quilting thread,
possible as pretty trimmings
or laces on one's boots.

Fallen

I made angels once
of knit and cotton wings,
constructed clouds of polyester fleece
pinned to blue fabric heaven.

I set angels on stationary froth
alone or in pairs only to have them
tumble earthward the entire day.

No matter the angels' restoration
in their still, celestial sphere,
they fell like window jumpers,
thudding on a flat surface.

How could angels behave so
corporeally,
fall with such decision from
fabric Heaven?

Is it my fault then, to have
placed them in a fabric sky
without one hint of stars?

Fire Sign (Leo Super Moon)

Snow moon in the sign of Leo
burns incandescent orange.
Clouds around it form a
halo made of fire.
Super in its orbit, it seems
close enough to touch;
orange, golden, butter,
phasing into brilliant white.

Its energy exponentially charged,
a lion crouched to leap,
now is the time for change,
time to manifest burning desires,
slash claws, with corded limbs,
the heavens and the earth.

Full Pink Moon

The moon is full and pink
before Easter, blushing amid
stars, planets, the Pleiades.

She portends blossoms with
her rose hue—butterflies and
newborn grass.

A pink pearl casting light
on Earth's return to life.
Sprouting Grass Moon,

Egg Moon the color of surprise
she knows about redemption,
victory over death.

Pink as new flesh,
she gleams like an ascending soul.
Winter is just the stone she rolls away.

Stardust

We are atoms and energy,
wavelengths of cosmic dust
glittering starshine paths
behind us across time and space.

Earth, rocks, trees,
hearts of those we love,
even aural fields of strangers
experience our vibrations
as we pass.

Why does the weight of skin
make us forget?

Its false boundaries bind us
muscle, sinew, bone
to a third dimension of
deadlines, dead weight, dead ends.

Encased in micro metered elasticity
proven harder than a shell,
our true natures spin and vibrate,
seethe to fly beyond a finite cage.

What more do we need to
remind us we are
finer materialized beings traversing
this coarse dimension?

We are stardust, energy
pulsing through the very
veins of God.

Damned

Bill was sitting in his bathtub
when the Rapture came,
his atoms vibrating fast enough for God.
His being lifted skyward . . . til he
realized he was nude.

Plopped back to the physical,
Bill surveyed the soapy
slop on his linoleum
in dismay.

I was cleaning out the pool
when he relayed his fate to me.
"You might as well stay with us
sinners," I said, sweeping and sweating,
my flesh around me like wet clothes.

Unconsoled, Bill moaned of
God's impatience, bad luck,
and discomfort at eternity
in the raw.

I saw no reason to voice
the odds of clothes
or bodies for souls
sucked up to Heaven like leaves
through a hose.

Who knows?

Bill felt foolish
enough as it was,

dropping with doubt from
God's redemption,
and I can't kick a man
when he's damned.

Psychic Lace

Say we leave tendrils of emotions,
shimmering behind us like snail paths
every place we traverse.
Crisscrossed loops of iridescent energy,
yards of psychic lace
continue beyond us for eons,
remnants left by every   single   soul.

Most fibers too fine to see
in a blue moon, happenstance,
sometimes brush a face or fingertips, and
one of us pauses to take note.

Scents of roses, a room that makes us blue,
or anger bubbling from nowhere
through our auras like errant electricity,
they could be traces of generations past,
threads of hope, knots of disappointment,
embellishments of grief,
all part of this gossamer brocade
we weave together.

Is this then the veil of tears?

Heartbreak in Heaven

Is there heartbreak in Heaven
when those few valiant souls depart,
descend like dandelion seeds
into matter's dense frequency,
sprout and root in bodies
borrowed for a blink
that lasts life spans?

What of the spirit clan left behind?

Permeated as they are in Collective Soul,
they have insights,
glimpses into Akashic libraries
of every story told
or ever to be told.

In a non-temporal plane
the departed have merely
stepped into another room,
will return in heart beats,
arms laden with stargazer lilies,
baby's breath, and briar,
    "Look what we found this time."

Strolling in God's gardens
arm in astral arm,
even that clan must feel some ache,
long for the return of wandering
loved ones.

Or do they simply watch over them
patient as mothers with their children
and find that is enough?

Bread of Life

The toaster pops up Christ's visage
scorched golden into bread.
"This is my body," he said once
and requested ritual remembrance.

Now he appears on toast or
grilled cheese sandwiches,
sells on eBay to the faithful.
He is still the bread of life,
thank God.

Miracles must arrive abbreviated
like text messages and emoticons,
Jesus on a pancake,
His eyes heavenward.

"Love ye one another," His browned face pleads.
"Take this toasted bread, eat of it."
No one can scroll past a pancake,
but will His missive stick?

Will we remember to do unto others
as we would have done unto ourselves?
Or will we toss Jesus
butter-side down
and walk away?

About the Author

Brenda Leigh White is a native Emporian whose heart resides on acreage of the family farm in Morris County, Kansas. An ex-opera student and cloth dollmaker, she is prone to talking to herself, to animals, and the occasional inanimate object. Her hobbies are daydreaming and watching snails.

White is a graduate of Emporia State University. Her work has appeared in *Quivera* and *The Flint Hills Review*. She writes poetry out of necessity.

About the Cover Artist

Lacy Auchard is a multi-media artist living in Madison, Kansas, whose work is strongly influenced by Nature. She works in ceramics, in colored pencil, watercolor, and ink drawing and has created fiber pieces as well. Her goal is to continue learning new ways to create art. Lacy graduated from Emporia State University with a BFA.

Acknowledgments

A big thank you goes to Curtis Becker who invited me to join the Emporia Writers Group, the beginning of it all. I owe Tracy Million Simmons for having faith in my work greater than my own. Her editing, formatting, and optimism built this manuscript. Cheryl Unruh encouraged me to share my voice. My family gave me support and, most importantly, time and encouragement to write my poems. Lacy Auchard contributed her beautiful art and constant friendship. I am forever indebted to Christopher Howell for his considerable and invaluable mentorship. And to the Emporia Writers Group, I extended my deepest thanks for their contributions, feedback, support, and friendships. You all mean so much to me.

www.birdypoetryprize.com

Meadowlark Press created The Birdy Poetry Prize to celebrate the voices of our era. Cash prize, publication, and 50 copies awarded annually.

The Birdy is an annual competition.

Final Deadline for Entries: December 1, midnight.

Entry Fee: $25

All entries will be considered for standard Meadowlark Press publishing contract offers, as well.

Full-length poetry manuscripts (55 page minimum) will be considered. Poems may be previously published in journals and/or anthologies, but not in full-length, single-author volumes. All poets are eligible to enter, regardless of publishing history.

See www.birdypoetryprize.com for complete submission guidelines. Also visit us at meadowlark-books.com.

Meadowlark POETRY

Books are a way to explore, connect, and discover. Poetry incites us to observe and think in new ways, bridging our understanding of the world with our artistic need to interact with, shape, and share it with others.

Publishing poetry is our way of saying—

*We love these words,
we want to preserve them,
we want to play a role in sharing them
with the world.*

www.ingramcontent.com/pod-product-compliance
Lightning Source LLC
Chambersburg PA
CBHW020911080526
44589CB00011B/547